Harriet Tubman

Leading Slaves to Freedom

Debra J. Housel

Consultant

Glenn Manns, M.A.
Teaching American History Coordinator
Ohio Valley Educational Cooperative

Publishing Credits

Dona Herweck Rice, *Editor-in-Chief*; Lee Aucoin, *Creative Director*; Conni Medina, M.A.Ed., *Editorial Director*; Jamey Acosta, *Associate Editor*; Neri Garcia, *Senior Designer*; Stephanie Reid, *Photo Researcher*; Rachelle Cracchiolo, M.A.Ed., *Publisher*

Image Credits

cover Cornell University Library/Library of Congress; p.1 Cornell University Library/Library of Congress; p.4 The Granger Collection; p.5 Cornell University Library; p.6 Library of Congress, LC-DIG-ppmsca-13305; p.7 The Bridgeman Art Library; p.8 Library of Congress, LC-USZC4-2525; p.9 Adisa/Shutterstock; p.10 The Granger Collection; p.11 The Granger Collection; p.12 The Granger Collection; p.13 Library of Congress, LC-USZ62-40247; p.14 (top) Library of Congress, (bottom) Library of Congress, LC-USZC4-4550; p.15 Library or Congress; p.16 The Granger Collection; p.17 Library of Congress, LC-USZ62-15887; p.18 Library of Congress, LC-USZC4-2519; p.19 Library of Congress, LC-USZ62-39380; p.20 The Granger Collection; p.21 Library of Congress, LC-USZ62-7816; p.22 Library of Congress, LC-USZC4-2519; p.23 The Granger Collection; p.24–25 The Granger Collection; p.26 Getty Images; p.27 Anthony Pleva/Alamy; p.28 (left) Adisa/Shutterstock, (right) The Granger Collection; p.29 (left) Library of Congress, LC-USZC4-2519, (right) The Granger Collection; p.32 Zuma Press/Newscom

Teacher Created Materials
5301 Oceanus Drive
Huntington Beach, CA 92649-1030
http://www.tcmpub.com

ISBN 978-1-4333-1603-6

Printed by: 926. Printed in: Malaysia. PO#: PO16413

Table of Contents

From Slave to Leader

Harriet Tubman was a brave woman. She was born a **slave** on a Maryland (MAIR-uh-lund) **plantation** in about 1820. When Harriet grew up she ran away. She joined the fight against slavery. She led many slaves to freedom.

A slave running away from his master

Harriet Tubman

A Young Slave Girl

Harriet was one of 11 children. Her family lived in a one-room hut. It had a dirt floor and no windows. At age 5, Harriet worked in the fields. At age 7, she cared for a white baby day and night. At about age 12, Harriet saw a slave running from his master. Runaway slaves were punished.

A slave hut

A slave child watches over a sleeping white child while sewing.

Slaves were treated badly.

To help the man get away, Harriet stepped between him and his master. The angry master threw an iron. It hit Harriet in the head. She almost died. She did not wake up for weeks. When Harriet did wake up, she decided she wanted to be free.

Harriet's owner would not spend money on a doctor for her.

An old iron weighs more than 7 pounds.

A Daring Escape

In 1844, Harriet married John Tubman. He was a free **African American** man. She told him she planned to run away. One night in 1849, she escaped. She took three of her brothers with her. But her brothers got too scared. They went back.

Slaves hiding at night

Before Harriet married John, her master died. Then she was sold to another master.

Men, women, and children waiting to be sold

Harriet ran away. She went to a white woman's house. The woman was part of the **Underground Railroad**. The Underground Railroad had no tracks. It had no trains. It was made up of people who wanted to help slaves. The people helped runaway slaves travel north to freedom.

One stop on the Underground Railroad

Fun Fact

Thomas Garrett hid slaves behind a wall in his shoe shop. He helped 2,700 people.

Thomas Garrett

The Fugitive Slave Act of 1850 let runaway slaves in the North be taken back to slavery.

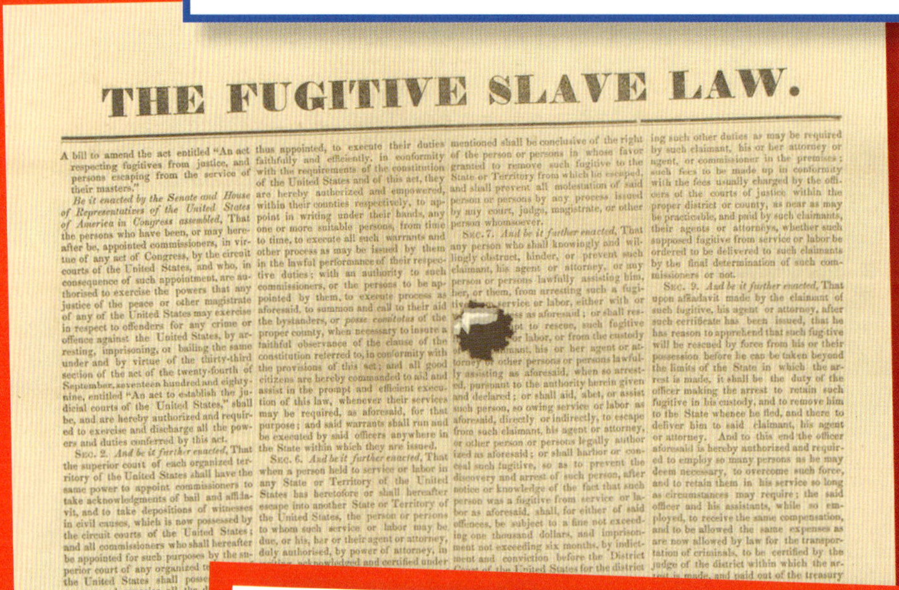

THE FUGITIVE SLAVE LAW.

A bill to amend the act entitled "An act respecting fugitives from justice, and persons escaping from the service of their masters."

Be it enacted by the Senate and House of Representatives of the United States of America in Congress assembled, That the persons who have been, or may hereafter be, appointed commissioners, in virtue of any act of Congress, by the circuit courts of the United States, and who, in consequence of such appointment, are authorised to exercise the powers that any justice of the peace or other magistrate of any of the United States may exercise in respect to offenders for any crime or offence against the United States, by arresting, imprisoning, or bailing the same under and by virtue of the thirty-third section of the act of the twenty-fourth of September, seventeen hundred and eighty-nine, entitled "An act to establish the judicial courts of the United States," shall be, and are hereby authorized and required to exercise and discharge all the powers and duties conferred by this act.

SEC. 2. *And be it further enacted,* That the superior court of each organized territory of the United States shall have the same power to appoint commissioners to take acknowledgments of bail and affidavit, and to take depositions of witnesses in civil causes, which is now possessed by the circuit courts of the United States; and all commissioners who shall hereafter be appointed for such purposes by the su-

...

thus appointed, to execute their duties faithfully and efficiently, in conformity with the requirements of the constitution of the United States and of this act, they are hereby authorized and empowered, within their counties respectively, to appoint in writing under their hands, any one or more suitable persons, from time to time, to execute all such warrants and other process as may be issued by them in the lawful performance of their respective duties; with an authority to such commissioners, or the persons to be appointed by them, to execute process as aforesaid, to summon and call to their aid the bystanders, or *posse comitatus* of the proper county, when necessary to insure a faithful observance of the clause of the constitution referred to, in conformity with the provisions of this act; and all good citizens are hereby commanded to aid and assist in the prompt and efficient execution of this law, whenever their services may be required, as aforesaid, for that purpose; and said warrants shall run and be executed by said officers anywhere in the State within which they are issued.

SEC. 6. *And be it further enacted,* That when a person held to service or labor in any State or Territory of the United States has heretofore or shall hereafter escape into another State or Territory of the United States, the person or persons to whom such service or labor may be due, or his, her or their agent or attorney, duly authorised, by power of attorney, in

...

mentioned shall be conclusive of the right of the person or persons in whose favor granted to remove such fugitive to the State or Territory from which he escaped, and shall prevent all molestation of said person or persons by any process issued by any court, judge, magistrate, or other person whomsoever.

SEC. 7. *And be it further enacted,* That any person who shall knowingly and willingly obstruct, hinder, or prevent such claimant, his agent or attorney, or any person or persons lawfully assisting him, her, or them, from arresting such a fugitive [illegible] service or labor, either with or [illegible] as aforesaid; or shall rescue [illegible] to rescue, such fugitive [illegible] or labor, or from the custody [illegible] claimant, his or her agent or attorney [illegible] other persons or persons lawfully assisting as aforesaid, when so arrested, pursuant to the authority herein given and declared; or shall aid, abet, or assist such person, so owing service or labor as aforesaid, directly or indirectly, to escape from such claimant, his agent or attorney, or other person or persons legally authorized as aforesaid; or shall harbor or conceal such fugitive, so as to prevent the discovery and arrest of such person, after notice or knowledge of the fact that such person was a fugitive from service or labor as aforesaid, shall, for either of said offences, be subject to a fine not exceeding one thousand dollars, and imprisonment not exceeding six months, by indictment and conviction before the District

...

ing such other duties as may be required by such claimant, his or her attorney or agent, or commissioner in the premises; such fees to be made up in conformity with the fees usually charged by the officers of the courts of justice within the proper district or county, as near as may be practicable, and paid by such claimants, their agents or attorneys, whether such supposed fugitive from service or labor be ordered to be delivered to such claimants by the final determination of such commissioners or not.

SEC. 9. *And be it further enacted,* That upon affidavit made by the claimant of such fugitive, his agent or attorney, after such certificate has been issued, that he has reason to apprehend that such fugitive will be rescued by force from his or their possession before he can be taken beyond the limits of the State in which the arrest is made, it shall be the duty of the officer making the arrest to retain such fugitive in his custody, and to remove him to the State whence he fled, and there to deliver him to said claimant, his agent or attorney. And to this end the officer aforesaid is hereby authorized and required to employ so many persons as he may deem necessary, to overcome such force, and to retain them in his service so long as circumstances may require; the said officer and his assistants, while so employed, to receive the same compensation, and to be allowed the same expenses as are now allowed by law for the transportation of criminals, to be certified by the judge of the district within which the ar-

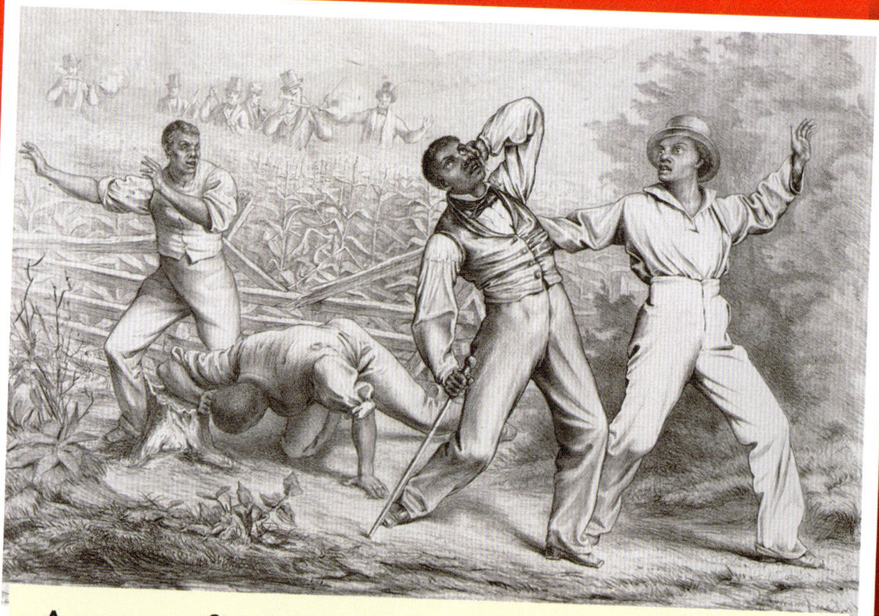

A group of men being brought back to slavery

Harriet hid in homes or barns during the day. She walked at night. At last she crossed the **Mason-Dixon Line**. This line was the border between Pennsylvania (pen-suhl-VAY-nee-uh) and Maryland. North of this line was freedom. South of the line was slavery.

Mason-Dixon Line

Leading Others to Freedom

In Pennsylvania, Harriet met **abolitionists** (ab-uh-LISH-uh-nists). She joined their work against slavery. Harriet saved money. She used the money to go back to the South. She led slaves to the North. She did this 19 times and led more than 300 slaves to freedom.

Runaway slaves on their way to freedom

Fun Fact

People called Harriet Moses. Like Moses in the Bible, she led people out of slavery.

Frederick Douglass, an American abolitionist

Slave owners knew about Harriet. Posters offered money for her **capture**. But no one caught her. Harriet made herself look like a man or an old woman. She hid with the runaway slaves in swamps filled with snakes and snapping turtles. Harriet and the runaway slaves were cold and hungry.

A slave hiding in a swamp

A $12,000 reward was offered for Harriet's capture. This was a huge amount at that time.

$100 REWARD!

RANAWAY

From the undersigned, living on Current River, about twelve miles above Doniphan, in Ripley County, Mo., on 2nd of March, 1860, A NEGRO MAN, about 30 years old, weighs about 160 pounds; high forehead, with a scar on it; had on brown pants and coat very much worn, and an old black wool hat; shoes size No. 11.

The above reward will be given to any person who may apprehend this said negro out of the State; and fifty dollars if apprehended in this State outside of Ripley county, or $25 if taken in Ripley county.

APOS TUCKER.

A reward poster for the capture of a runaway slave

Harriet would not let runaway slaves turn back. She knew they would be punished. She also worried that they might tell someone about the Underground Railroad. If a runaway slave wanted to go back, Harriet pointed a gun at the person. She said, "Go on or die."

Harriet leading slaves to freedom

Fun Fact

Harriet never fired the gun. She never lost a person to slave catchers.

Serving the Union Army

The **Civil War** began in 1861. The states in the North fought the states in the South. The North wanted to free the slaves. Harriet worked for the **Union Army** in the North. She was a nurse and a **spy**. As a spy, she risked her life to pass secrets to the troops.

Many African Americans, both slave and free, fought for the Union Army.

Harriet worked for the Union Army for more than two years. She was never paid a penny.

One night in 1863, Harriet helped lead 150 African American soldiers up a river in South Carolina. In the darkness, they ruined enemy supplies. They freed nearly 800 slaves. And they did it without even one injury!

Harriet's mission was a success!

Fun Fact

All slaves were freed when the Civil War ended in 1865.

Harriet's Later Years

Harriet moved to New York. She gave land to her church to build a poorhouse. Harriet worked for women's right to vote, too. In 1913, Harriet died. She had risked her life dozens of times, but she lived to be 93.

Fun Fact

Local Civil War veterans gave Harriet a military funeral.

Harriet Tubman

Harriet Tubman monument

Time

1820

Harriet Tubman is born on a Maryland plantation.

1833

Harriet nearly dies of a head injury.

1849

Harriet escapes to Pennsylvania and becomes an abolitionist.

Line

1861

Harriet works as a nurse for the Union Army and frees slaves.

1863

Harriet spies for the Union Army during the Civil War.

1913

Harriet dies at the age of 93.

Glossary

abolitionists—people who work to put an end to unfair laws, such as slavery

African American—Americans whose families first came from Africa to the United States

capture—to catch a person in order to keep him or her somewhere

Civil War—an American war between the northern and southern states

Mason-Dixon Line—the division between free states and slave states

plantation—a large farm where crops are grown

slave—a person who belongs to another person and must work for no money

spy—a person whose job is to find out secret information about another country or group

Underground Railroad—a secret group of people who helped slaves escape

Union Army—the army of the northern states

Index

Americans Today

In 1987, Oral Lee Brown visited a first-grade class. The students were poor. She told them that she would pay for them to go to college. Each year she saved $10,000. Then she started the Oral Lee Brown Foundation. People gave money to help. Almost all of the students in the class finished college. Oral led them out of poverty.